Contents

Any words appearing in the text in bold, **like this**, are explained in the Glossary.

Why do people play musical instruments?

People around the world play musical instruments for different reasons. A few play or teach music for their jobs. They have spent many hours practising and playing to get better. They understand their instruments very well. However, most people play music just because they like it. They enjoy making sounds for their own or other people's pleasure.

Playing an instrument such as the clarinet can bring pleasure to others as well as to yourself.

FROM THE EXPERTS

"Music washes away from the soul the dust of everyday life."
Berthold Auerbach, German writer

"It's easy to play any musical instrument: all you have to do is touch the right **key** at the right time and the instrument will play itself."
J.S. Bach (1685–1750), famous composer, who found it very easy to play instruments!

Learning Musical Instruments

Should I Play the
Clarinet?

Richard Spilsbury

www.heinemann.co.uk/library
Visit our website to find out more information about Heinemann Library books.

To order:
 Phone 44 (0) 1865 888066
 Send a fax to 44 (0) 1865 314091
Visit the Heinemann Bookshop at www.heinemann.co.uk/library to browse our catalogue and order online.

First published in Great Britain by Heinemann, Halley Court, Jordan Hill, Oxford, OX2 8EJ, part of Harcourt Education.

© Harcourt Education Ltd 2007
The moral right of the proprietor has been asserted.
First published in paperback in 2008.

Editorial: Nancy Dickmann and Sarah Chappelow
Design: Richard Parker and Manhattan Design
Picture Research: Melissa Allison and Natalie Gray
Production: Camilla Crask
Illustrations: Jeff Edwards
Originated by Modern Age
Printed and bound in China by Leo Paper Group

The publishers would like to thank Teryl Dobbs for her assistance in the preparation of this book.

ISBN 978 0 431 05783 5 (hardback)

11 10 09 08 07
10 9 8 7 6 5 4 3 2 1

ISBN 978 0 431 05791 0 (paperback)

12 11 10 09 08
10 9 8 7 6 5 4 3 2 1

British Library Cataloguing in Publication Data
Spilsbury, Richard
  Should I play the clarinet?. - (Learning musical instruments)
  1.Clarinet - Juvenile literature 2.Clarinet music - Juvenile literature
  I.Title
  788.6'2

A full catalogue record for this book is available from the British Library.

Acknowledgements
The publishers would like to thank the following for permission to reproduce photographs:
Alamy pp. **4** (Jeff Greenberg), **18** (Visions of America, LLC); Bridgeman Art Library p. **7** (The Quartet - Jean Pierre Dupont (1741-1808) Pierre Vachon (1731-1803) Rodolphe, Provers and Vernier (w/c on paper), Carmontelle, (Louis Carrogis) (1717-1806)/Musee Conde, Chantilly, France, Lauros / Giraudon); Corbis pp. **20** (Reuters), **26** (Ariel Skelley); Getty Images pp. **14**, **22** (Lawrence Lucier), **23**, **27** (Mel Yates); Harcourt Education Ltd/Tudor Photography pp. **5**, **8**, **9**, **10**, **12**, **13**, **24**, **25**; Lebrecht pp. **15** (Graham Salter), **21** (G. Anderhub); Rex Features p. **6** (Image Source); Robert Harding p. **16** (Neil Emmerson); The Image Works p. **17** (Bob Daemmrich); TopFoto p. **19**.

Cover image of Don Byron playing the clarinet at the Monterey Jazz Fesstival reproduced with permission of Corbis/Craig Lovell.

Music and feelings

Music is a bit like a language that lots of people understand. When we play or listen to music, we may feel happy, thoughtful, or sad. We can even forget what we are actually doing. We may imagine different worlds or think about important things in our lives.

Music and getting together

Playing and listening to music is enjoyable because people do it together. You can share the experience of music making in **bands** or **orchestras**. You can make music in the classroom or with friends at home.

Learning to play an instrument takes time but is well worth the effort.

Music and learning

Many people believe that playing an instrument helps you learn other things. For example, studying the lives of **composers** helps you learn about history. The main thing you learn, though, is that playing music is lots of fun!

What is a clarinet?

A clarinet is a **woodwind** instrument. It is shaped like a narrow tube. You play it by blowing in one end through a pointed **mouthpiece**. The mouthpiece has a thin piece of bamboo called a **reed** in it.

You hold a clarinet with two hands, left above right. You change notes by pressing fingers over holes or against metal keys.

CLARINET FACTS: What are clarinets made of?

Like some other woodwind instruments, clarinets are usually made of wood. Particular types of hard, black wood from tropical forests – such as grenadilla – were always used in the past. They gave the clarinet a good sound. Today, many clarinets are made of special plastic instead. It is cheaper than wood.

History of clarinets

People have played woodwind instruments for thousands of years. The clarinet developed from an instrument of the early 1600s called the chalumeau (we say "shall-oo-mow"). This had a reed tied over a large hole in the mouthpiece. It had seven holes and one **key** for the player to change **notes**.

In 1690 Johann Denner changed the chalumeau. He added more keys to play more notes. He made it longer and widened the end. He moved the reed to the underside of the mouthpiece. His invention was called the clarinet. It has remained very similar since then, but extra keys have been added. Now it can play even more notes!

This painting shows a clarinet being played as part of a quartet in the 1700s. The other instruments are a cello, a French horn, and a violin.

The parts of a clarinet

This is a top view of a clarinet showing the main parts, what they are called, and what they are for. On the underside of the clarinet (not visible in the photograph), there are other important parts. This is where we find the reed, the register key, and the thumb rest. The register key is operated using the thumb. It is used to play very high notes. The thumb rest rests on the right-hand thumb when playing. This helps the player to support the instrument.

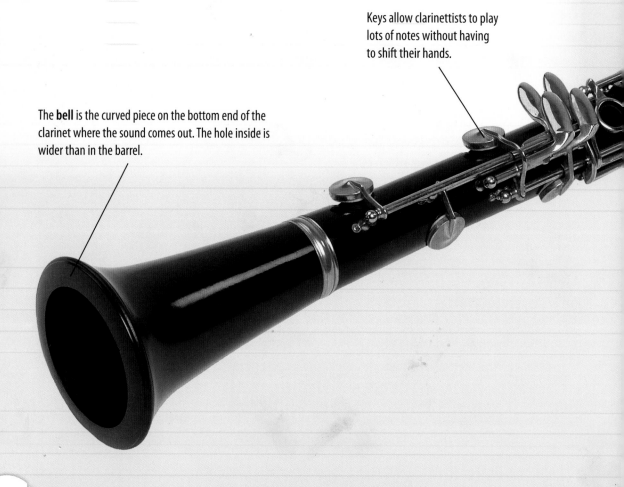

Keys allow clarinettists to play lots of notes without having to shift their hands.

The **bell** is the curved piece on the bottom end of the clarinet where the sound comes out. The hole inside is wider than in the barrel.

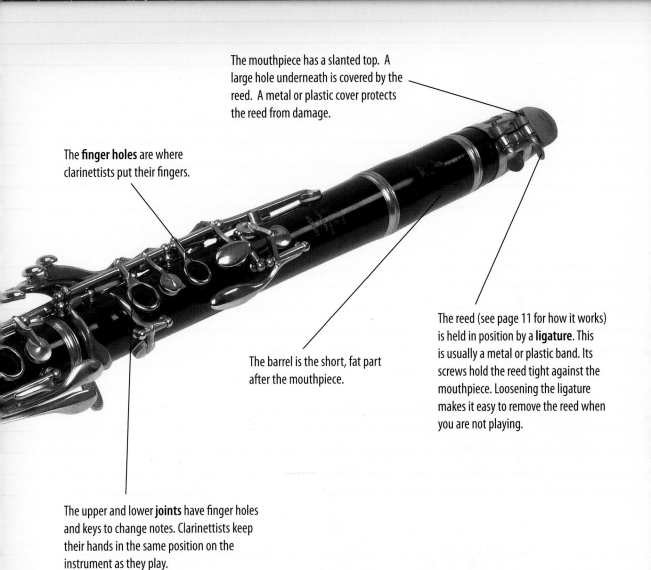

The mouthpiece has a slanted top. A large hole underneath is covered by the reed. A metal or plastic cover protects the reed from damage.

The **finger holes** are where clarinettists put their fingers.

The reed (see page 11 for how it works) is held in position by a **ligature**. This is usually a metal or plastic band. Its screws hold the reed tight against the mouthpiece. Loosening the ligature makes it easy to remove the reed when you are not playing.

The barrel is the short, fat part after the mouthpiece.

The upper and lower **joints** have finger holes and keys to change notes. Clarinettists keep their hands in the same position on the instrument as they play.

How does a clarinet make its sound?

Making sound waves

Have you ever blown across the top of a bottle to make a sound? Sounds happen when something **vibrates**. The air inside a bottle vibrates when we blow across it. Air inside a clarinet vibrates when you blow into the **mouthpiece**. The vibrations travel out in all directions, a bit like the ripples that spread after you drop a pebble in a pond. The waves of vibrating air are called **sound waves**. We hear sound waves as **notes** when they reach our ears.

Blowing across the neck of bottles with different amounts of water creates different notes.

Changing notes

The note or **pitch** a bottle makes gets higher if you put water inside. That's because the water leaves less space for air. A shorter length of air vibrates faster than a longer length. The sound waves are closer together. We then hear a higher pitch.

We change pitch on a clarinet by covering or uncovering holes. This changes how much air there is inside. The clarinet produces its lowest pitch when all the holes are closed. This is the longest possible length of air it can hold.

A clarinet reed bends up and down 29 times each second when you blow over it!

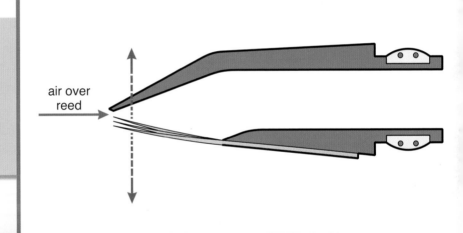

air over reed

CLARINET FACTS: How does a reed work?

A **reed** starts and controls the vibration of the air inside the clarinet. As you blow over a reed, the power of the air makes its tip bend up and down again and again. This happens fast and regularly. The regular movement of the reed keeps the air vibrating to make a clear sound. Reeds work best when they are moistened in water or in your mouth before playing.

Covering the holes

Clarinet players cover **finger holes** with their fingertips. They use both fingertips and knuckles to press **keys**. Each key is attached to a lever. The lever presses a felt pad firmly over a hole, covering it. Springs move the pad off the hole once the key is released. On many clarinets, most of the finger holes have metal rings over them. The rings operate as keys. They open or close other holes when particular **fingering** is used.

You can see how the length of air inside shortens as more finger holes are uncovered.

Playing beautiful notes

A good **embouchure** (we say "om-boo-shoor"), or mouth position, helps to produce a beautiful sound. It can also help you reach very high notes. You fold your lower lip over your lower teeth, bite gently on the mouthpiece, smile slightly and blow! It sounds tricky, but practice can help you get it right.

Breathing right

Clarinettists should always blow air into the mouthpiece from their lungs, not from puffed-out cheeks. They can blow for longer and play longer notes. When you puff out your cheeks, your lower lip gets floppy. It then vibrates with the reed as you play. This affects the sound you make.

The best way to play a clarinet is to stand or sit up straight. Hold the instrument pointing downwards, about halfway between horizontal and vertical. This position helps you breathe better than if you are slouched.

It is important to stand up straight to play the clarinet.

FROM THE EXPERTS: THE CLARINET SOUND

"The voice of the Swan, singly, is shrill, piercing and harsh, not unlike the sound of a clarinet when blown by a novice [beginner] in music."

Thomas Bewick, *History of British Birds, 1809*

Which musical family are clarinets from?

The clarinet is one type of **woodwind** instrument. Other familiar woodwinds are the flute, oboe, saxophone, and bassoon.

Family sound

We group musical instruments into families by how they make their sounds. Most woodwinds use **reeds** to create sound. Oboes and bassoons have two reeds which flap together when blown. Flute players blow across a hole, rather like blowing across a bottle, to get the air inside **vibrating**. Brass instruments such as the trumpet are another family of blown instruments. Brass players vibrate their lips rather than a reed to get a sound.

The tenor saxophone is a woodwind instrument with a single reed like the clarinet.

CLARINET FACTS: Metal woodwind instruments

The first woodwind instruments were always made of wood. Today, flutes and saxophones are made of metal instead. The saxophone is the most recent woodwind instrument. It was invented by Adolphe Sax in the 1840s. Its **keys** and fingering are similar to a clarinet's. The saxophone first replaced oboes and bassoons in military **marching bands**. It could play a wider range of notes. Today, saxophones are widely used in **jazz** music.

Different clarinets

Most people play the B flat **soprano** clarinet. There are about 13 less common types, including:

- The E flat **alto**. This produces slightly different **pitches** using the same **fingering** as the soprano.
- The sopranino clarinet. This is the shortest clarinet. It can play very high **notes**.
- The bass clarinet. This has a curved neck and **bell**. The bell lengthens the air inside, so it can play very low notes.
- The rare octocontrabass clarinet. This is over 2 metres (6 feet) tall. It has a leg at the bottom to support its weight. It makes the lowest notes of any clarinet.

The bass clarinet is over twice the size of a soprano clarinet.

This man is playing an instrument similar to the *midjweh* in Goa, India.

Reed instruments around the world

There are many less familiar types of instruments with reeds. The *midjweh* is from Egypt. It is traditionally made out of reeds from the banks of the River Nile. It is like two very simple oboes tied together. *Midjweh* players blow both **mouthpieces** at once. They cover two **finger holes** at once. This means they play two notes at a time.

The *bin* is the instrument played by snake charmers. Its mouthpiece is made from a hollowed-out gourd (type of hard squash). The mouthpiece has a reed inside.

The *shehnai* is a type of North Indian oboe. It has two reeds inside and a double reed in the mouthpiece. This gives a special buzzing sound to the notes. **Bands** with *shehnai* players are often hired to play at weddings. Their music is thought to bring good luck to the newly married couple.

What types of music can you play on a clarinet?

Of all the **woodwind** instruments, the clarinet makes probably the widest range of sounds. It can play low **notes** and high notes. Its sounds range from smooth and gentle to honks and shrieks. Clarinets are common in **marching bands**, **orchestras**, and **jazz** and **folk** groups. The clarinet is not used much in rock music. It isn't loud enough to compete with the electric instruments usually found in a rock **band**.

 Many orchestras, including some school orchestras, have a group of clarinettists in their woodwind section.

Marching band music

For hundreds of years, music was used in battles. It encouraged troops and put off their enemies. The clarinet was probably first used in military bands in the middle of the 1700s. Like flutes and drums, clarinets were easy to carry and play while marching. People also put on concerts of military band music. One of the most famous **composers** of this music in the 1800s was John Philip Sousa.

Today marching bands are still popular. The only time they go into battle is in competitions with other bands! A typical marching band has many clarinettists. Its other woodwind instruments include saxophones and flutes.

Marching bands can be huge. Can you spot the clarinettists in this US marching band?

This is a Dixieland jazz band playing in New Orleans, USA.

Classical or orchestral music

Classical composers first wrote clarinet parts for orchestras in the late 1700s. Many of the best early players had been trained in military bands. The famous Austrian composer Wolfgang Amadeus Mozart loved the sound of the clarinet. He wrote a very famous clarinet concerto in 1791. It is still often played today. He also wrote many pieces for smaller groups that included clarinets. There have been clarinettists in most orchestras since Mozart's time.

Jazz and folk

Jazz is a type of music with a strong rhythm. It is partly written and partly **improvised**. Clarinets have been used in jazz since it first developed in the southern United States about 100 years ago. They are used regularly in traditional or Dixieland jazz groups. These groups play versions of tunes first written by New Orleans bands. Piano, drums, and a double bass or tuba often provide the **backing**. Trumpets and clarinets play **solos**. The saxophone is more popular than the clarinet in much jazz today. However, plenty of modern jazz still features clarinets.

Folk music is the traditional popular music shared and known within a community. The clarinet is used in different types of folk music, including **klezmer.** Travelling Jewish musicians in Eastern Europe developed this style in the 1800s. Klezmer groups usually include a clarinet. It can sound like someone singing with joy or sadness.

CLARINET FACTS: The famous "glide"

George Gershwin's *Rhapsody in Blue* of 1924 starts with some of the most famous clarinet music ever written. It contains a long note that glides smoothly from low to high. This sound makes some people think of looking up at the skyscrapers in New York, the city where Gershwin lived. There is a story that the glide was not in the *Rhapsody* when Gershwin first wrote it. Clarinettist Ross Gorman was messing around in rehearsal. He played the glide instead of the separate notes written down. Gershwin liked the sound so much he put it in the final version!

Klezmer acts are often part of the Jazz Festival in Hollywood, USA. This event features some of the world's best jazz musicians.

Who plays the clarinet?

The best clarinettists in the world bring something extra to their music, whatever the style.

Classical clarinettists

Jack Brymer (1915–2003) was a famous British **classical** clarinettist. He played with lots of **vibrato**, which means **pitches** that waver up and down slightly. Jack taught himself on his father's old **alto** clarinet. When he was young, most clarinet music was written for **soprano** clarinet. He could not afford to buy one, so he sawed a bit off the alto to make it the right length!

Sabine Meyer is a top classical clarinettist. Many modern **composers** have written music especially for her **woodwind** group.

FROM THE EXPERTS

"When I was 4, I heard the clarinet and asked my mom if I could have one. She thought it was a passing interest."

Julian Bliss - By the time he was 15, Julian was so good at the clarinet he had already performed around the world and made his first CD!

CLARINET FACTS: Reviving the clarinet

Don Byron was born in New York in 1958. He listened to all sorts of music – pop, jazz, symphonies, and ballet. Don is mostly a jazz clarinettist. He also writes music for children's shows, string quartets, dancers, and films. His music is influenced by anything from hip-hop to klezmer. He has helped to make the clarinet popular again.

Jazz clarinettists

Sidney Bechet (1897–1959) began playing with top New Orleans **bands** at the age of 11. He had fantastic clarinet **technique** and great ideas for **improvising** tunes. Benny Goodman (1909–1986) was probably the best-known clarinettist of the early 20th century. His **orchestra** played a **jazz** style called swing. It was great for dancing. People everywhere heard his music on radio shows and recordings. Swing became less popular in the 1950s. The saxophone became the major jazz woodwind instrument.

FROM THE EXPERTS: ON GIORA FEIDMAN

"He is simply one of the best clarinettists around, with his ability to speak, laugh, and cry through his instrument."

Simon Broughton, *Rough Guide to World Music*

Klezmer

The first **klezmer** clarinet star was Naftule Brandwein (1889–1963). He was one of millions of Jews who left Eastern Europe for the United States in hope of a better life. Naftule could not read music, but he played with great speed and energy. The most famous living klezmer clarinettist is Giora Feidman. He played classical music with the Israel Philharmonic Orchestra for 20 years. Then he switched to traditional klezmer music.

Some modern groups combine klezmer with other styles of music. For example, the Klezmatics group plays traditional klezmer tunes. They use African drums or even electric guitar **solos** as well.

Giora Feidman has won many awards for his clarinet playing.

How would I learn to play the clarinet?

Many people buy their own clarinets. There are lots of types for sale. Plastic clarinets are usually cheaper than wooden ones. Secondhand instruments are cheaper than new ones. Music teachers or clarinettists can help you choose a beginner's clarinet. They may tell you what to look for in a clarinet, such as **keys** that move easily. They may even recommend a particular type of clarinet. Make sure the instrument you choose has a secure case. This will protect it when you carry it around.

CLARINET FACTS: On hire

Some people hire a clarinet for a short time before buying it. Hiring is cheaper than buying. It gives you the chance to decide whether the clarinet is the right instrument for you. It also lets you try different types of clarinets.

It is important to try out different clarinets before choosing one.

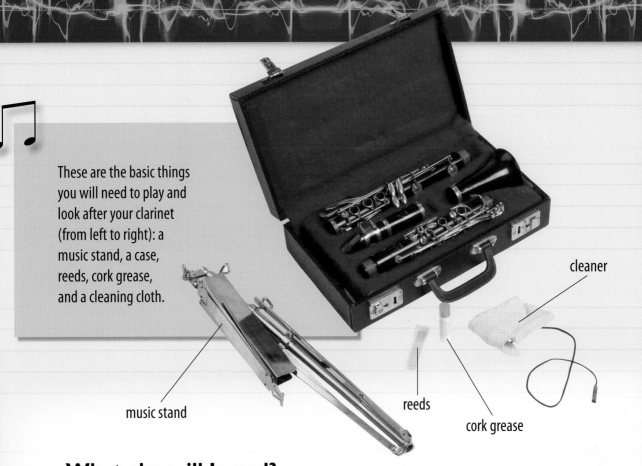

These are the basic things you will need to play and look after your clarinet (from left to right): a music stand, a case, reeds, cork grease, and a cleaning cloth.

cleaner

music stand

reeds

cork grease

What else will I need?

The clarinet cannot make a sound without a **reed**. Reeds come in different hardnesses or strengths. Beginners usually start with number 2 reeds. Their softer tips are easier to **vibrate** than harder ones. Clarinettists often switch to harder reeds as they improve their blowing. These reeds give a better sound. Reeds get soggy and wear out after playing for a few weeks, so you will need some spares.

Other important items include a fluffy cleaning swab, cork grease, and a clarinet stand. The swab mops up the moisture you leave inside your instrument when you blow. The grease helps the cork around the ends of the clarinet parts fit together easily. The stand holds your instrument upright when you need to put it down. This position is safer for the clarinet than laying it flat. You can get a music stand to hold your music as you play.

Learning

Some of the best clarinettists taught themselves. However, most people do best learning clarinet with a teacher. Teachers will help you to read clarinet music and develop a good **embouchure**. They will show you which **fingerings** to use for different **notes**. They can also prepare you for music exams.

You may find a teacher by asking at your school. You can look at adverts in your local library or music store. Ask other clarinettists or music teachers if they can recommend someone. Some people have lessons during the school day. Others have lessons at home.

CLARINET FACTS: Playing in groups

It is great fun to play in groups of clarinettists and other wind instruments. You can join a school **marching band**, wind **band**, or **orchestra**. You will learn a lot in a group. You can watch what other clarinettists do and listen to the sounds they make.

A good teacher will quickly understand what help you need in order to play the clarinet better.

It takes lots of practice and time to improve on any instrument.

Getting better

Taking lessons and playing in groups help you to learn. It is also important to practise at home. Many people practise at the same time each day, in the same quiet place. They may have a routine of playing some **scales** and some pieces each time.

Always remember that playing should be fun, not a chore. Even scales can feel worthwhile if you try to play them as beautifully as possible. You can watch and listen to good clarinettists playing music on TV, radio, CDs, and in concert. This will help to develop your sound.

Recordings to listen to

Classical

Mozart's Clarinet Concerto in A Major played by Jack Brymer with the Royal Philharmonic Orchestra, conducted by Thomas Beecham (EMI)

Benny Goodman's Collector's Edition bundles together Bernstein's *Prelude, Fugue and Riffs* and Copland's *Clarinet Concerto*. It also includes some other good clarinet pieces played by Benny Goodman with the Columbia Symphony Orchestra, conducted by Leonard Bernstein (Sony).

The Essential Clarinet features pieces similar to those above, played by modern American clarinettist Richard Stoltzman (RCA).

Music for Clarinet and Piano played by Julian Bliss is one of his first CDs. It demonstrates his talents at the age of 15 (EMI).

Check out the opening of Gershwin's *Rhapsody in Blue*!

Jazz

The Best of Sidney Bechet (Blue Note) features Sidney Bechet on clarinet and on **soprano** saxophone.

Complete RCA Victor Small Group Master Takes (Definitive) by Benny Goodman was originally recorded in 1935–39. Benny plays even better here than on many of his swing orchestra CDs.

Tony Scott's *Music for Zen Meditation* (Polygram) is a very relaxing mix of gorgeous clarinet with Japanese instruments such as bamboo flute.

Music for Six Musicians (Nonesuch) by Don Byron displays his talent for creating unique music.

Napoli's Walls (ECM) by Louis Sclavis is a classic modern jazz clarinet CD.

Klezmer

Byron, Don, *Don Byron Plays the Music of Mickey Katz* (Elektra Nonesuch) shows again how well this clarinettist can play different styles of clarinet music.

Feidman, Giora, *Magic of the Klezmer* (Delos)

Statman, Andy, *The Hidden Light* (Sony)

The Klezmatics *Rhythm + Jews* (Piranha)

Timeline of clarinet history

1690   Johann Denner invents the clarinet

1712   French **composer** Estienne Roger writes the earliest-known music for the clarinet

1716   Clarinet is used in an **orchestra** for the first time, in Vivaldi's *Juditha Triumphans*

1770   The bass clarinet is invented in Paris

1780   Most orchestras include a pair of clarinettists

1785   Separate **mouthpiece** is developed

1791   Mozart's clarinet concerto is first performed

1812   Ivan Mueller invents airtight, leather-covered pads so **keys** close up holes properly

1831   All clarinet mouthpieces have the **reed** on the bottom rather than on the top

1840s   Adolphe Sax invents the saxophone

1840   The Klosé-Buffet clarinet is developed, with movable rings around the **finger holes** and 17 keys

1869   The first clarinet reeds are made by machines. Before this all reeds were cut by hand.

1889   **Klezmer** clarinettist Naftule Brandwein is born

1894   Brahms composes his famous **classical** clarinet sonatas

1909   Benny Goodman is born

1915   Classical clarinettist Jack Brymer is born

1924   Gershwin composes *Rhapsody in Blue*

2005   Classic FM poll puts Mozart's clarinet concerto as most popular classical piece

Glossary

alto type of instrument which produces lower notes than a soprano one

backing supporting the soloist

band organized group of musicians

bell wider end part of a woodwind or brass instrument

classical formal style of music, usually written for orchestral instruments

composer person who writes music, often either writing it down or playing it first

embouchure mouth shape that helps woodwind players get a good sound

finger hole hole in a woodwind instrument that is opened or closed with a finger

fingering use of particular fingers or combinations of fingers to play notes on an instrument

folk range of musical styles from different places, based on traditional, popular tunes

improvise make up music as you play it

jazz style of music with strong rhythm that is part composed and part improvised

joint main part of a clarinet. The instrument has an upper and lower joint.

key lever used to change a note on a musical instrument

klezmer style of Jewish or eastern European folk music

ligature band holding the reed to the mouthpiece

marching band band in which musicians play as they march along

mouthpiece part of an instrument which is blown into to play it

note musical sound (single pitch) made by an instrument or voice

orchestra large group of musicians divided into groups of string, brass, woodwind, and percussion instruments

pitch speed of vibration of sound waves producing a particular note

reed thin strip of material such as bamboo that vibrates when blown to make a noise

scale set of musical notes arranged in order of pitch

solo play without accompaniment

soprano type of instrument which produces higher notes than an alto one

sound wave moving pulse of air we hear as sound

technique method of playing

vibrate to move back and forth at a particular speed

vibrato playing technique which produces a varying pitch

woodwind family of instruments played by blowing air across holes or over reeds. These include the clarinet and saxophone.

Further resources

Books

Abracadabra Clarinet: The Way to Learn Through Songs and Tunes,
   Jonathan Rutland (A&C Black, 2002)

Illustrated Book of Musical Instruments, Max Wade-Matthews (Southwater, 2005)

Making Musical Instruments from Junk, Nick Penny (A&C Black, 2005)

Making Music: How to Create and Play Seventy Homemade Musical Instruments,
   Anne Sayre-Wiseman and John Langstaff (Storey Kids, 2003)

The Complete Theory Fun Factory, Kate Elliot and Ian Martin
   (Boosey & Hawkes, 1996)

The Magnificent I Can Read Music Book, Kate Petty and Jenny Maizels
   (Bodley Head Children's Books, 1999)

The Rough Guide to Clarinet, Hugo Pinksterboer (Rough Guides, 2001)

Saxophone & Clarinet: An Easy Guide to Reading Music,
   Chris Coetzee (New Holland Publishers, 2004)

Sound Effects, M. J. Knight (Franklin Watts, 2005)

DVD

See one of the greats of the past playing:

Benny Goodman, *Adventures in the Kingdom of Swing* (2000)

Websites

The Philharmonia Orchestra in UK hosts a website that introduces orchestral instruments and lets you hear them being played in classical orchestral pieces. http://www.philharmonia.co.uk

Find a list of registered clarinet teachers in your area at: http://www.ism.org/registers.php

Index